Metal Molds
Ice Cream, Chocolate, Barley Sugar & Cake

By Eleanore Bunn

Photographs by Pierre Jarige

COLLECTOR BOOKS
P.O. Box 3009
Paducah, KY 42001

The current values in this book should be used only as a guide. They are not intended to set prices, which vary from one section of the country to another. Auction prices as well as dealer prices vary greatly and are affected by condition as well as demand. Neither the Author nor the Publisher assumes responsibility for any losses that might be incurred as a result of consulting this guide.

Additional copies of this book may be ordered from:

COLLECTOR BOOKS
P.O. Box 3009
Paducah, Kentucky 42001

@ $5.95 Add $1.00 for postage and handling.

Copyright: Eleanore Bunn, 1981
ISBN: 0-89145-175-7

This book or any part thereof may not be reproduced without the written consent of the Author and Publisher.

Printed by IMAGE GRAPHICS, Paducah, Kentucky

Acknowledgements

My thanks to my family and the many friends who encouraged or prodded me toward the completion of the book. To Theodore and Florence Williams, Betty Bonvouloir, and Sue Brigham, who provide pleasurable companionship and transportation on collecting trips. To Beverley Brule, treasure hunter supreme, who alerts me to interesting finds. To a flea market stranger who overheard me say I planned to write this book and quipped, "That's what they all say, but they never do". That chance remark ended my procrastination. The writing began.

My thanks to the many dealers who supplied information and either allowed or donated pictures: Mrs. Ella Sonntagg of East Hartford, CT and Mrs. Haines of The Brown Jug, Sandwich, MA, who sold me my first ice cream mold and gave me help in finding much needed information.

My very particular thanks to Polly and Charles Gaupp of The House of The Clipper Ship, East Sandwich, MA. Mrs. Gaupp was most friendly in encouraging the examination of her fine and extensive collection of ice cream molds, sharing her knowledge and expertise, and allowing photography. Their collection also includes the unusual display models of the ice cream shapes, originals from Krauss, as pictured in the book. Here also I acquired copies of old Eppelsheimer and Krauss catalogues (reprints) which have been invaluable in research.

My very special thanks also to Barbara Ray and her family who opened their home to me and Mr. Jarige to photograph her own private collection. Mrs. Ray has been collecting and selling molds for many years. The examples photographed are the special rare ones she has kept for her own collection. To enjoy her family and her hospitality and be allowed to photograph her collection was a privilege.

A final thanks to Judy Gaillardetz, who suggested the photography of Pierre Jarige. His fine photography, an art form in itself, turns a book of facts into a visual pleasure.

The photographs of molds from The House of The Clipper Ship are adaptations of photographs by Stephanie Curtis.

Table of Contents

Acknowledgements	3
Introduction	5
Prices	6
Pewter Ice Cream Molds	7
Chocolate Molds	41
Hard Candy or Barley Sugar Molds	72
Cake Molds or Pans	75
Unusual Molds	78
Fascination of and Uses for Collections	79
Bibliography	80

Introduction

We usually associate sculpture with marble, museums, public buildings, or lavish homes and gardens, but not with things we eat. For more than 200 years sculptors have been shaping the figures from which molds are made for ice cream, chocolate, candy and cake. Some of the forms are realistic, some crude, some stylized, and some whimsical. Most are finely detailed. All show the skills of the sculptors and designers.

These molds have become very popular antiques and collectibles. Their popularity relates (as do most antiques) not only to their charm but also to their nostalgia. Years ago, ice cream Santa Clauses with white beards, red suits and dark boots stood in nests of sparkling spun sugar to delight children at Christmas when the ice cream was served for dessert. Barley sugar candy images - bears, elephants, dogs, musical instruments, etc. -adorned the Christmas tree or formed lollipops. The Easter Bunny, when he filled the Easter baskets, nestled a chocolate rabbit in the basket with the jelly beans and marshmallow chicks.

"The Hall of Everyday Life in the American Past" in the Smithsonian Institution in Washington, D.C. has a permanent display of an old-time ice cream and candy store with ice cream and chocolate molds and replicas of the finished ice creams (Figures 1, 9, & 10). (An Eppelsheimer catalogue of metal ice cream molds shows these colored models of the molds instead of the actual molds themselves. The company indicates there was a demand for these models which confectioners could keep in their show cases or supply to their salesmen as samples of the finished ice creams.) The fixtures and ice cream and chocolate molds in the museum are from Stohlman's Confectionary Shop, Georgetown, D.C., circa 1900. They are the gift of J. William Stohlman.

For Mr. Duncan B. Walcott, who worked for Borden in Akron, Ohio, collecting ice cream molds was "sort of a busman's hobby" according to "Spinning Wheel". Certainly he is the foremost authority. The Dearborn Museum has ice cream molds from his collection.

As people search for molds today, they enjoy their interesting forms and shapes, and many searchers also are flooded with childhood memories and nostalgia.

Prices

All prices indicated in the illustrations are approximate estimates of antique dealers' figures. It would be extremely difficult to determine specific worth because many factors are involved. A dealer who collected a mold for $5.00 may be selling it for less than one which had been purchased later for $20.00. Time, place, subject, condition, and desirability all play a part. For example: The chocolate rabbit mold (Figure 131) was priced at one antique show for $22.00 and a year later at another show for $35.00. At that time, the same mold was purchased for $15.00 in a Chicago suburb where a candy store was selling them out.

Within 5 years, the Griswald cast-iron rabbit cake mold (Figure 164) at antique shows has had price tags of $25.00, $50.00, and finally $100.00 for one that was in very poor condition. In the past year, the author has bought ice cream molds from $18.00 each for a complete collection to a high of $70.00 for one specially rare and appealing mold, the Indian Chief. The average prices have been between $25.00 and $55.00. Similar price differences were found in chocolate molds as indicated by two simple tray molds: one priced at $8.00, the other at $23.00.

Certainly prices are rising, but in the last analysis in the market of antiques and collectibles, price is determined by what the seller is asking and the buyer is willing to pay. Prices may be found above or below suggested price ranges.

Pewter Ice Cream Molds

Ice cream molds were used commercially, not in homes, so they are not usually found in old attics or barns. The collector must search the antique shows and shops, flea markets, or auctions. Early collectors can remember picking up individual size molds (6-8 to the quart) for $2.00 to $5.00. The prices then went to $10.00, $20.00, and $25.00 and have continued to climb steeply depending on condition and subject. Larger molds - 1½ pints or more - were used less than the individual ones so they are very scarce. Such large molds may include: Santa (Figure 2), rabbits, railroad engines, baskets, horses, ships, birds, dogs, cats, or elephants. Very few of these remain on the market, and their prices may run to hundreds of dollars. Single very small ones - usually fruit or flowers used to fill baskets - still may be found in the $15.00 range.

The forms of ice cream molds are varied because different shapes were used for holidays and parties. For example: at Christmas there were Santas (Figures 11-15), Christmas trees (Figure 16), poinsettias, and holly; at Halloween, witches (Figure 64), witch's cats (Figure 65), and pumpkins (Figures 25 & 26); at Thanksgiving, Pilgrims, horns of plenty (Figure 22), turkeys (Figure 47), or Indians (Figure 52); at Easter, rabbits (Figures 44-46), flowered crosses, and chickens (Figure 48). For weddings there were flowers, wedding bells (Figure 66), hearts (Figure 68), cupids (Figure 55), and engagement and wedding rings (Figure 67); for children's parties, trains, cars (Figure 74) and animals; and for fraternal orders, the symbols of the orders.

Other models are sport figures (Figure 56) such as baseball and football players, bicyclists, and golfers; patriotic figures such as George Washington (Figure 54), Uncle Sam, and the Liberty Bell; fruits such as apples or pears; and flowers, including orchids (Figure 38), lilies (Figures 37 & 39), roses (Figures 31-34), rose buds (Figure 35), daisies (Figure 42), asters (Figure 41) and pansies (Figure 43).

There are also unusual or unlikely subjects such as a log, a tree, a slice of watermelon (Figure 71), a roasted turkey (Figure 69), beehive, asparagus, salt cellar, phone, frog, poached egg, skull, potato, etc.

An old Krauss catalogue lists 27 animals, 35 flowers, 15 fruits, and 32 birds. An old Eppelsheimer catalogue lists 39 animals, 41 flowers and leaves, 51 fruits, and 36 birds.

Illustrations of Duncan B. Walcott's extensive collection, which in 1965 contained 984 different examples, 186 of which were one of a kind, indicate that divisions can be made into separate categories. Ships: ark, ocean liner, battleship, racing yacht, clipper ship and Santa Maria; sports figures: bicyclist, golfer, and football and baseball players; Civil War: knapsack, cannon, soldier, sailor, and drum; horses: two different heads, rocking horse, race horse with jockey, rearing horse and circus horse. A large mold of a rearing horse also was made.

Mr. Walcott cites the 1799 inventory of William Will, a Philadelphia pewterer, as including pewter ice cream molds, so they were available almost 200 years ago. Individual ice cream shapes were most popular from the mid 1800's, when commercially made ice cream first became available to the mid 1900's. In a 1965 article, Mr. Walcott states that a few companies were still making them for custom order, but for children today the ice cream Santas are no longer available or are exceedingly rare. No longer will the counter, filled with a selection of pewter molds with a big pewter railroad engine resplendant on top, be seen at the caterer's. Probably two things brought about this change—lead in pewter molds which was proclaimed dangerous, and more important, the work necessary to produce the individual ice cream figures. The Health Department of the City of New York, fearing the danger of lead poisoning, banned the use of lead in ice cream molds in that area.

An Eppelsheimer catalogue lists ice cream molds of "99% Pure Block tin" (sometimes molds were so marked) at 20% above their other prices which range from $1.50 to $2.50 in this catalogue. A Krauss catalogue lists the same price difference for tin molds. These tin molds could replace the pewter ones where they were banned.

Three molds (Figures 16, 21, 67) from the New York area are tin washed copper, whether related to the ban is not known. Information on them is limited and they are less desirable to collectors.

In 1965, Duncan B. Walcott wrote that Fr. Krauss Son, Milford, PA, was still making molds using 61% tin and 39% lead. It is doubtful if pewter ice cream molds are made today. The materials are costly and the demand is almost non-existent.

Packing the individual molds was a hand process, not a machine process, since different colors of ice creams were used to give a natural effect. For example: a daisy would be white with a yellow center; a watermelon slice perhaps would have pistachio ice cream for the rind, raspberry sherbet for the inside part, and chocolate seeds.

An Eppelsheimer catalogue, which lists metal molds and their colored models, gives the following information on coloring the shapes:

> "**Color Effects** are obtained by using different flavored ice cream such as vanilla for white, Pistachio for green, Strawberry for pink, Chocolate for brown, and so forth. These flavors are pressed into the various parts of the molds with a small knife or spatula.
>
> **Coloring** is also done by Painting, Spraying or Dipping the hardened Ice Cream form into a certified food color.
>
> Color designs of rare beauty and attractiveness may be obtained by using one of the methods mentioned or a combination of them.
>
> The appearance of Ice Cream forms may be further improved by the addition of "fixtures" such as artificial leaves, flags, ribbons, and so forth, some of which are suggested throughout this catalogue."

As labor costs increased, the cost of such individual work became almost prohibitive and the continued manufacture impractical. Although they were never cheap, if you could custom order ice cream shapes today as possibly can still be done in New York City - the price would be exorbitant.

The catalogue also gives methods of freezing, storing and shipping the ice cream shapes. Freezing ice cream shapes was more difficult before refrigerators were invented. Electricity, however, was in use when the cataogue was printed since one mold is an early light bulb.

When the molds were no longer used, they were scrapped, discarded, or sold. An antique dealer had bought ice creams from the Hood Company and made an offer for all their molds when they stopped using them. Unfortunately the molds had been scrapped before the offer was received. Reputedly the Hershey chocolate molds were scheduled for a similar fate until an employee suggested that they might be sold. Thus that extensive collection ended in the collectors' field instead of on the junk heap. It is said that many French molds were melted for bullets during World War II. One of the last caterers to make ice cream shapes in the Boston area lost his molds in a fire. Lead melts very easily, and sadly his molds became molten lumps.

Rarely do you find a mold without some mark, usually the raised model number. The maker's mark is often not found or is hard to locate or read, because pewter is soft and the marks often wore down. Sometimes maker's marks were deliberately removed. After the Krauss Company bought out the Schall Company they removed the "S & Co." mark from the molds. The author's collection has two same-numbered Santas, one with the "S & Co." mark and the other with it filed off (Figure 11). Evidently the model number was considered most important.

Again, we are indebted to Mr. Walcott for the identity of many maker's marks. Schall and Company of New York City, one of the oldest U.S. mold makers established in 1854, marks their molds "S & Co." (Figure 24). Eppelsheimer and Company mark their pieces "E & Co.N.Y.".

Mr. Walcott found that the company J. Ernst, N.Y. (a charming pair of love birds so marked) was listed in the New York directories in 1858 and 1872 at different addresses. The "CC" mark was identified from an old U.S. catalogue of ice cream molds quoting prices on ice cream molds at $9.00 a dozen. On the back cover, the catalogue states, "Our molds are superior to the celebrated "CC" molds of Paris." A Paris city directory of 1904 verified the maker and the mark as M. Cadot et Cie of Paris founded in 1826. The "CC" mark (Figure 6) resembles "GG", and sometimes the mold also used an old hand-crank ice cream freezer trade mark. In 1904, *successors* was sometimes used with the company name and the words *Marque, Fabrique* or *deposee* (Figure 6).

S.G.D.G. (sand garantie du gouvernment) and Brevete' (patent) were also sometimes included as French marks and identify French molds. Flared hinges are also indicative of French molds.

Other marks may appear on American molds besides the usual model number and possible or probable maker's mark. An American Indian with no distinguishable maker's mark states "Des Cop'd. 1896" (Figure 52) (perhaps necessary because a cruder, unmarked similar mold was found). An "E & Co." lady states "Des. Cop'rd 1890" (Figure 58). Such dates are of course copyright dates, not manufacturing dates.

Fig. 1. Smithsonian Institution Photo #77-12067. Model of large Santa ice cream mold. Sample to show customers. Model shows use of different ice creams for color and the accessory of Christmas Tree. Probably Eppelsheimer #194. From the ice cream and candy store in "The Hall of Everyday Life in the American Past" (fixtures from Stohlman's Confectionery Shop), Smithsonian Institution, Washington, D.C. Original mold $300.00 - 400.00.

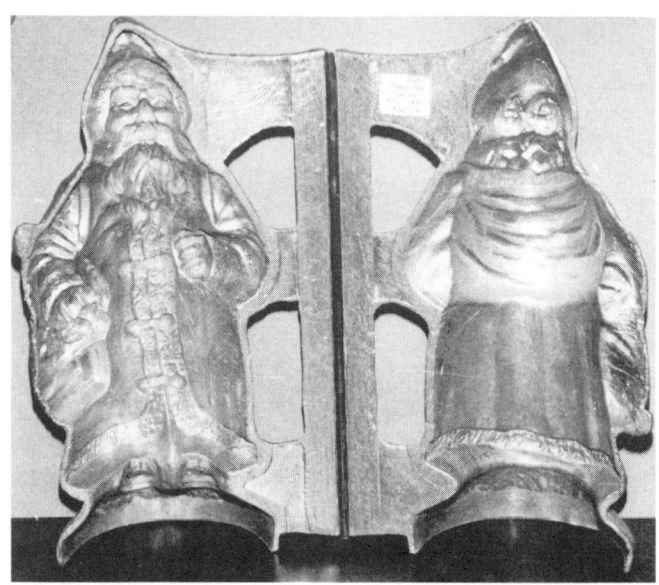

Fig. 2. Collection of House of The Clipper Ship. Interior of banquet size Santa Claus mold E & Co., #194. Rare, fine condition. $300.00 - 400.00.

g. 3. Collection of House of the
pper Ship. Banquet size ice
eam mold of duck, Krauss #44.
re, fine condition. $250.00
50.00.

g. 4. Collection of Barbara
y. Rare banquet size rooster
e cream mold. 11½". Mint con-
ion. $300.00 - 400.00.

Fig. 5. Collection of Barbara Ray. Banquet and individual size log ice cream molds. Banquet size, 10". $175.00 - 250.00. Individual E & Co. #987. $55.00.

Fig. 6. Collection of Barbara Ray. Banquet size basket. Marked "Brevete, SGDG, Remarque Fabrique, CC.". French flared hinges. Rare marking, good condition. $125.00 - 250.00.

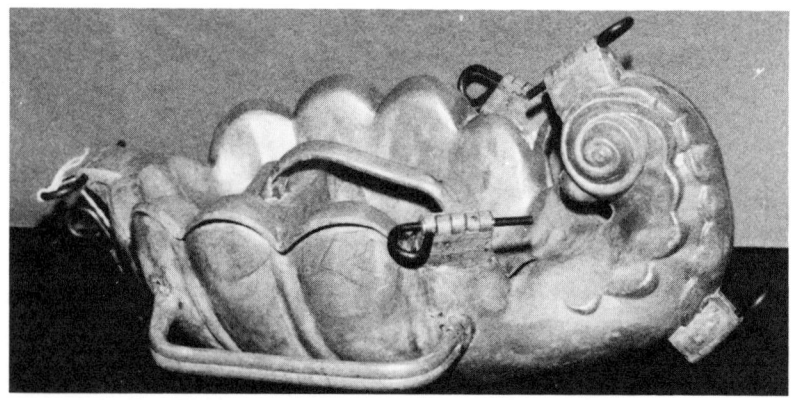

Fig. 7. Collection of House of the Clipper Ship. Banquet size, "base for shell", Krauss 36B. Lovely, rare. $200.00 - 300.00.

Fig. 8. Smithsonian Institution Photo #78-6006. Model of ice cream shape of ship from "The Hall of Everyday Life in the American Past" (fixtures from Stohlman's Confectioners Shop), Smithsonian Institution, Washington, D.C. Such battleships were made in the large sizes - 1½ to 2 quart, and in the individual size. Large size, $200.00 - 300.00; individual, $35.00 - 45.00. Rowboats, sailboats, the ark, etc. are additional individual boat molds. $35.00 - 75.00.

Fig. 9. Smithsonian Institution Photo #77-12068. Model of individual ice cream Santa shape with Christmas tree accessory. From the ice cream and candy store in "The Hall of Everyday Life in The American Past", (fixtures from Stohlman's Confectioners Shop). Smithsonian Institution, Washington, D.C. Original pewter mold, $35.00 - 45.00.

Fig. 10. Smithsonian Institution Photo #77-12071. Model of individual ice cream mold of Santa in his sleigh, pulled by reindeer. The reindeer antlers probably were added accessories. From the ice cream and candy store in "The Hall of Everyday Life in the American Past", (fixtures from Stohlman's Confectioners Shop), Smithsonian Institution, Washington, D.C. Rare, original mold. $45.00 - 65.00.

Fig. 11. Individual ice cream Santa mold interior. S. & Co. #427, later made by Krauss with "S & Co." removed. $35.00 - 45.00.

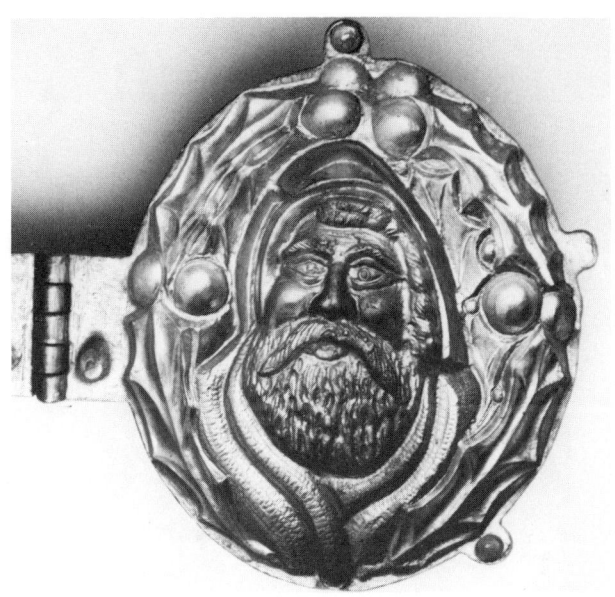

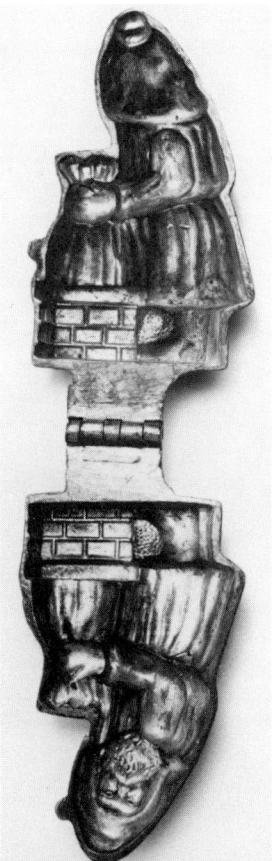

Fig. 12. Interior of individual flat, rounded ice cream mold of Santa wreathed in holly. Bottom is plain as is the entire exterior. No maker's mark. Number badly worn "8??" Unusual. $40.00 - 45.00.

Fig. 13. Interior of individual ice cream mold. Santa with his pack going down chimney. Marked "E + Co., N.Y., 1171". Rare, fine condition. $65.00 - 75.00.

Fig. 14. Individual ice cream mold interior. Santa going down chimney. Unmarked, exterior rather crude. Replacement hinge pin. Unusual. $45.00-50.00.

Fig. 15. Interior of individual Santa ice cream mold. Hinge worn with replacement pin. Not very detailed, but quaint. $40.00 - 45.00.

Fig. 16. Exterior of Christmas tree showing marking "641 K". This mold is not pewter, but tin-washed copper - evident where spots of plating have worn off. Interior is detailed and in mint condition. 40.00 - 45.00.

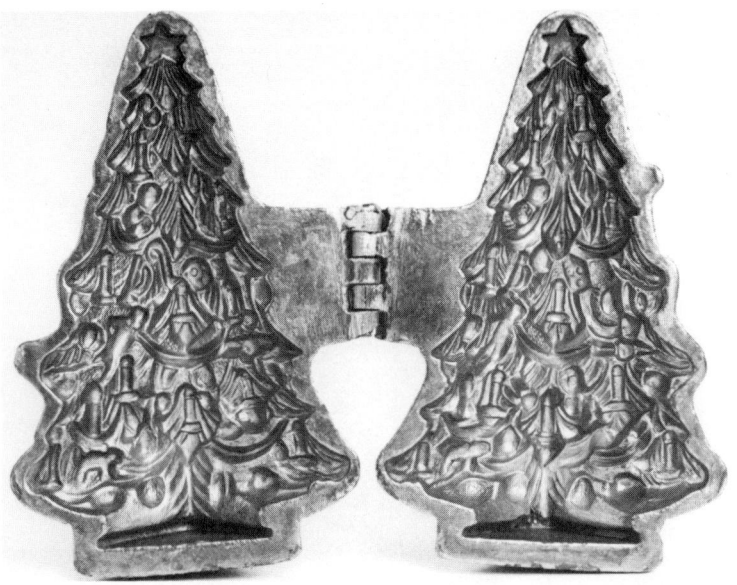

Fig. 17. Interior of Figure 16 showing fine detailing.

Fig. 18. Collection of Barbara Ra[y]. Very fine larger (5½") ice crea[m] mold wreath. Marked "E & C[o]. N.Y., 1146". Fine conditio[n]. $90.00-95.00.

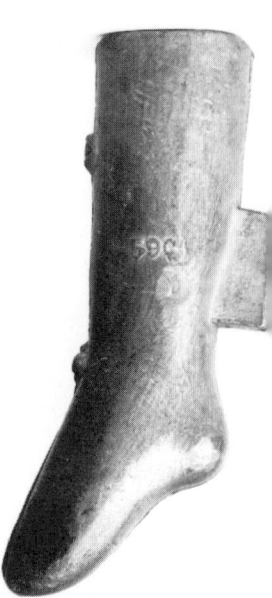

Fig. 20. Collection of Barba[ra] Ray. Christmas stocki[ng] marked "596". Fine and ra[re]. $75.00 - 85.00.

Fig. 19. Collection of Barbara Ray. Very unusual individual ice cream mold of Christmas fireplace marked "E & Co., N.Y. M1202". Rare and mint condition. $65.00 - 75.00.

Fig. 21. Individual ice cream mold of horn of plenty showing number "287" and worn areas. This mold is tin-washed copper, not pewter, and the plating has worn off in places. Interior condition is fine. $20.00-25.00.

Fig. 22. Collection of Barbara Ray. Fine pewter horn of plenty marked "E & Co., 1004". Excellent condition. $65.00 - 75.00.

Fig. 23. Collection of Barbara Ray. Flat Christmas bell mold. (See wedding bell Figure 66) #404. Rare. Fine condition. $55.00 - 65.00.

Fig. 24. Individual ice cream corn mold marked "S & Co., 270". Beautiful detail and condition. $40.00 - 50.00.

Fig. 25. Pumpkin mold, unmarked with unusual latch. Shows signs of wear. $30.00-35.00.

Fig. 26. Pumpkin very similar to Figure 25, but this is evidently newer -and is marked "600". This is the number in the Krauss catalogue, but the maker's mark has been filed off. (Krauss bought out Schall and often thus removed the "S & Co." mark.) Fine condition, not rare. $30.00-35.00.

Fig. 27. Lime ice cream mold. Marked "CC, 814, Brevete, SGDG". Early, good condition. $30.00-35.00.

Fig. 28. Grapes marked "159". No maker's mark, but this is a number for Krauss grapes. (Bunches of grapes were made also in smaller sizes or with leaves.) Condition good. $35.00 - 45.00.

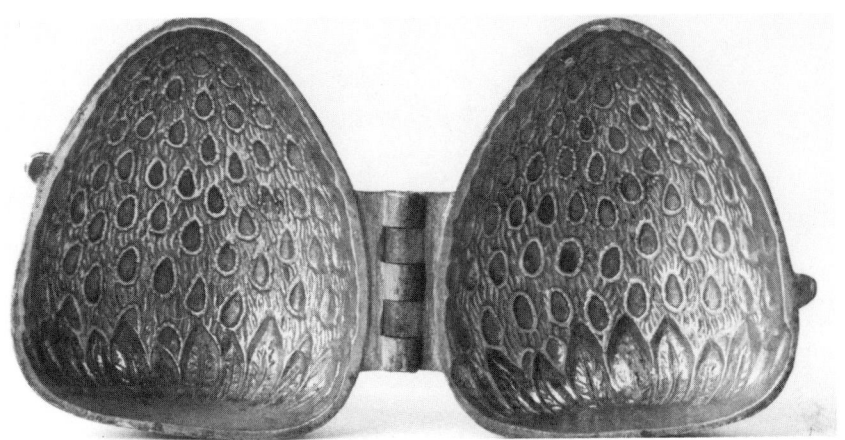

Fig. 29. Collection of Barbara Ray. Individual strawberry ice cream mold. Numbered "503", which is a Krauss number although there is no maker's mark. Rare and in mint condition. $60.00-65.00.

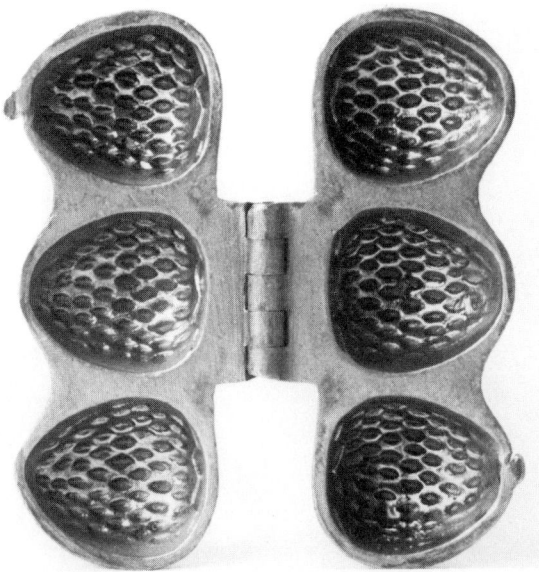

Fig. 30. Collection of Barbara Ray. Triple ice cream mold of small, natural-size strawberries marked "S & Co.". Mint condition. $50.00-55.00. Double and triple molds were made of other small objects such as apples, cherries (four in mold), eggs (three or four to mold), pansies, peaches, potatoes, pears, mushrooms, raspberries (four in mold), roses, walnuts, and shells.

Fig. 31. Rose numbered "582". No maker's mark, but this is the number for Krauss' American Beauty Rose. Prime condition. $45.00 - 50.00.

Fig. 32. Rare diminutive rose marked "CC", with widely flared French hinge. 1 3/8". Early, but in beautiful condition. $25.00 - 35.00. (A similar rose, full-blown, about 2" was also made. It's value would be $30.00 - 40.00).

Fig. 33. Three roses combined in individual mold. Markings are worn but number is possibly "391" which is Krauss number. Except for the worn mark, the mold is in good condition. $35.00 -45.00.

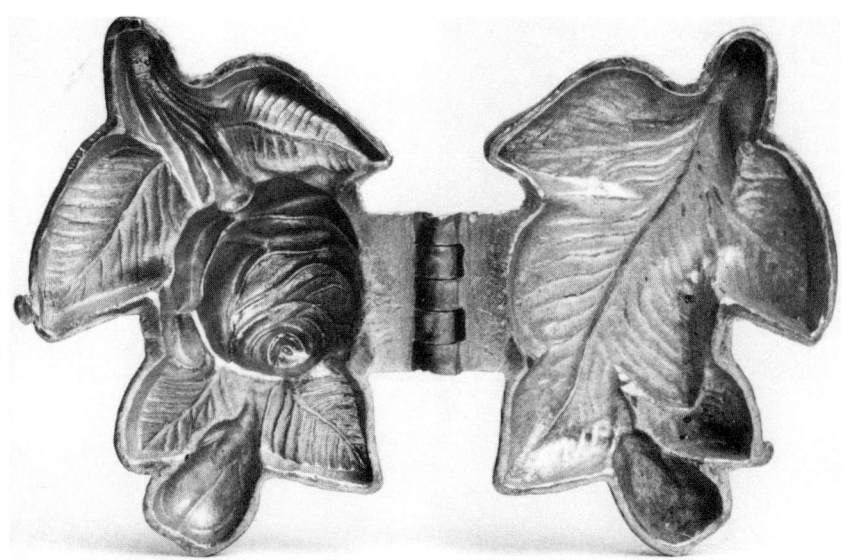

Fig. 34. Rose with leaves and bud. Beautifully detailed. Marked "S & Co.". $45.00 -55.00.

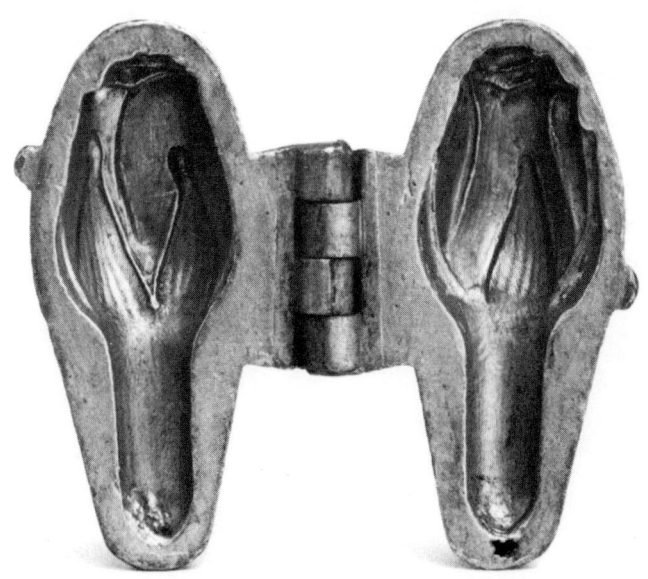

Fig. 35. 2½" rosebud mold (about natural size). Marked "CC" on each half. Early and rare. French flared hinge. Condition fine. $25.00 - 35.00.

Fig. 36. Box-shaped individual ice cream mold decorated with wild roses. No maker's mark. The number "455" is badly worn, but is the Krauss number for this pattern mold. Fine condition, useful as trinket box. $35.00 - 50.00.

Fig. 37. Three-piece, double hinged calla lily mold. Marked "S & Co., 210" and "Pat Apl'd For". Early and discolored from age, but beautiful and in fine condition. $45.00 - 50.00.

Fig. 38. Orchid mold marked "319 Des, cop'd 1892". No maker's mark. Condition fine. $55.00 - 65.00.

Fig. 39. Three-piece, double hinged lily mold. Marking seems to be "J.B." in two places. Seems to be early and a little crude on the outside. $25.00 - 35.00.

Fig. 40. Chrysanthemum marked "313". No maker's mark, but Krauss lists one under this number. A very handsome mold in fine condition. $45.00 - 55.00.

Fig. 41. Aster mold numbered "236". No maker's mark, but this is the number for Krauss for this pattern. Good condition. $35.00 - 45.00.

Fig. 42. Daisy mold marked "E & C N.Y., 317". (Similar small daisies w made three to a mold, #349.) Fin detailed on the interior, good con tion. $30.00 - 45.00.

Fig. 43. Flat pansy mold with stem. Number appears to be "269", a Krauss number for pansy. (A smaller one was made, #397). No maker's mark appears, the hinge is incised "C & G Co.", evidently the owners of the mold. Good condition. $30.00 - 45.00.

Fig. 44. Lying rabbit mold with worn number "190", a Krauss number, though there is no maker's mark. (The least rabbit - looking of all the rabbits.) Good condition. $30.00 - 45.00.

Fig. 45. Rabbit half standing. Krauss numbered "189", no maker's mark. $45.00-50.00. (Krauss also makes two smaller rabbits, #297 and #191). $35.00 - 45.00.

Fig. 46. Seated rabbit mold - probably the best designed of all the rabbits. Marked "E & Co., N.Y. 658". Also available in copper. $50.00 - 65.00.

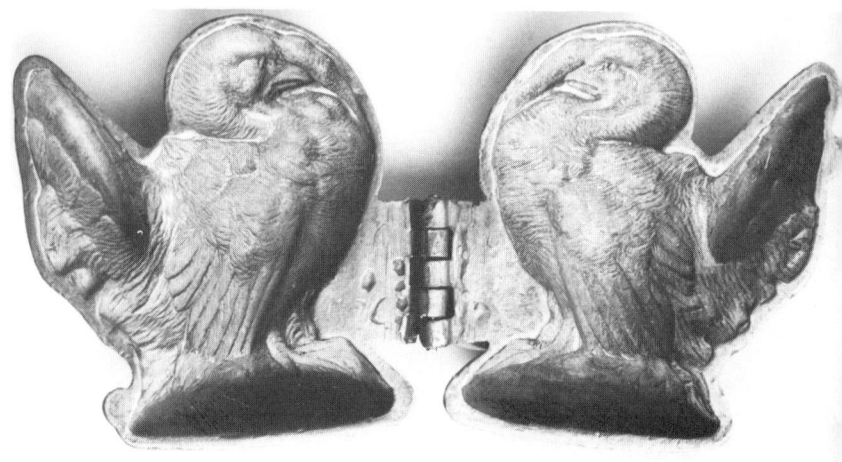

Fig. 47. Interior of individual turkey ice cream mold. Marked "E & Co., N.Y." Number is worn off, but should be "650". Good condition. $35.00 - 45.00.

Fig. 48. Chicken marked "E & Co., N.Y., 652". Early, good condition. $35.00 - 45.00.

Fig. 49. Dove of Peace in flight. Marked "E. & Co., N.Y., 677". Rare and beautiful mold. Fine condition. $65.00 - 85.00.

Fig. 50. Seated Dove of Peace with flowers. Marked "342", Krauss number, no maker's mark. $45.00 - 55.00.

Fig. 51. Duck marked "CC" on both halves. Flared French hinge. $40.00 - 50.00. (The same bird was made by Schall & Co. and later by Krauss #187.).

Fig. 52. Interior of Indian mold marked "458, Des. Cop'd 1896". No maker's mark. Krauss number. Beautifully detailed, rare. $70.00-75.00.

Fig. 54. Interior of George Washington mold. Marked "460". No maker's mark. Hinge incised "D & Co." fo owner's mark. Krauss' catalogue lists an accessory o hatchet on a wire. Good condition. $45.00 - 65.00.

Fig. 53. Dressed baby, marked "S & Co.", number "286". Early, rare, fine condition. $45.00 -55.00.

Fig. 55. Interior of Cupid mold. Marked "492". No maker's mark. Krauss number. For accessories, the Krauss catalogue lists gold or silver bow, arrow and wings. $45.00 -55.00.

Fig. 56. Smithsonian Institution Photo #78-6004. Interior of Girl on Bicycle (One of pair with Boy on bicycle). Rare. $50.00 - 65.00.

Fig. 57. Smithsonian Institution Photo #78-6001. Interior of Foxy Grandpa. Rare. $45.00-50.00.

Fig. 58. Old Mother Hubbard interior. Marked "E & Co., N.Y. 981 Des Cop'rd.1890". Rare. Fine condition. $60.00 - 70.00. Other storybook characters were also made. These are rare. $60.00 -75.00.

Fig. 59. Brownie, Eppelsheimer #1031. Has a fat stomach with double row of buttons. Rare. $60.00-65.00.

Fig. 60. Collection of Barbara Ra Teddy Bear marked "E & Co., N.Y 1103". Rare, fine condition. $65.0 -75.00.

Fig. 61. Engine and coal car showing numbers "477" and "478". $70.00-75.00 each.

Fig. 62. Collection of House of Clipper Ship. Complete train with passenger car numbered "479". $250.00 - 300.00 for set.

Fig. 63. Collection of Barbara Ray. Bunch of asparagus, unmarked miniature. $35.00 - 45.00.

Fig. 64. Witch on Broomstick, numbered "1153". No maker's mark. Listed in Eppelsheimer catalogue. Rare. $65.00 - 75.00.

Fig. 65. Collection of Barbara Ray. Witch's cat. Marked "E & Co., N.Y., 1175". Rare. Prime condition. $65.00 - 75.00.

Fig. 66. Wedding Bell. Krauss numbered "285". No maker's mark. Fine condition. $35.00 - 45.00.

Fig. 67. Engagement Ring. Marked "E & Co., 1141, K". (A matching wedding ring was also made.) Tin-washed copper, not pewter. $20.00-25.00. Pewter $45.00 - 55.00.

Fig. 68. Heart aflame marked "300", number for Krauss mold. Fine condition. $45.00 - 50.00.

Fig. 69. Roasted turkey, Krauss number "364". Hinge incised "D & Co.". No maker's mark, good condition. $35.00 - 40.00.

Fig. 70. Collection of Barbara Ray. Log. Marked "E & Co., 987". $50.00 - 60.00.

Fig. 72. Hobby Horse. Worn mark, "E Co.". Early, rare, fine condition. $65.00 -75.00.

Fig. 71. Collection of Barbara Ray. Watermelon slice. Marked "S & Co., 557". Early, fine condition. $55.00 - 65.00.

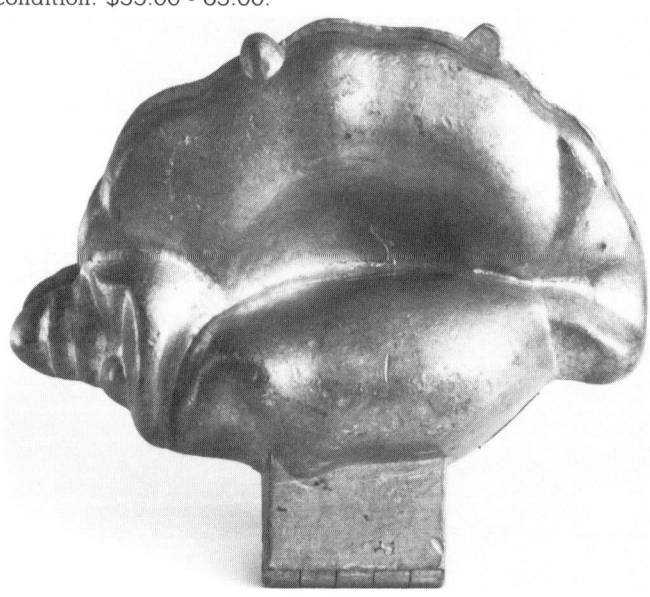

Fig. 73. Shell. Marked "S & Co.", number "311". Beautiful mold, remarkable condition. $60.00 - 75.00.

Fig. 74. Automobile, early, marked "S & Co., 562". $45.00 - 50.00.

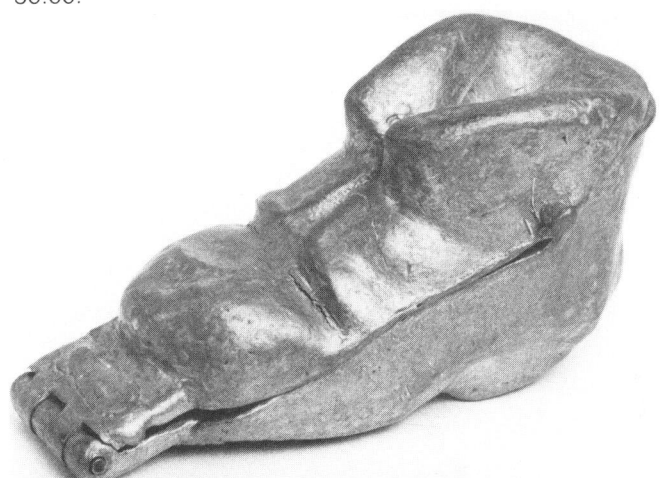

Fig. 75. Shoe. Worn condition. $30.00 - 50.00.

Fig. 76. Boat. Unusual since it is hinged at both ends, with the pin in the bow hinge removable. The same mold was later made with only one hinge. $35.00 -50.00.

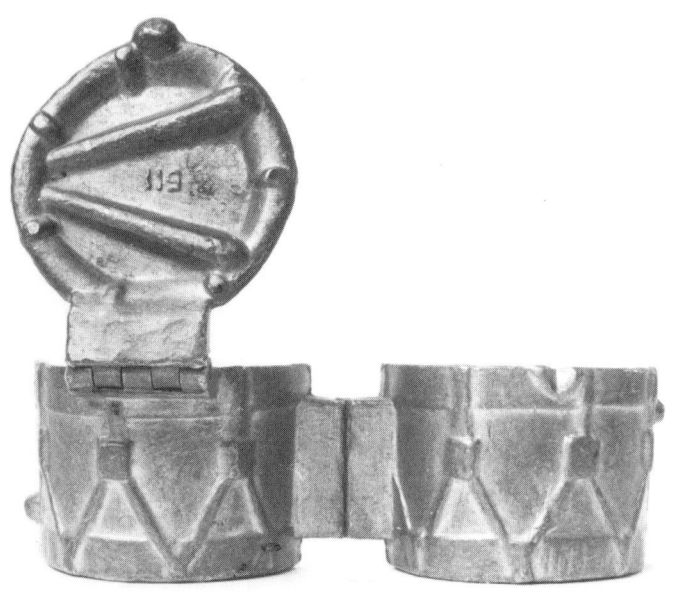

Fig. 77. Collection of Barbara Ray. Double-hinged, three-piece mold of Drum, Krauss, #511A. No maker's mark. Fine condition. $65.00 - 75.00.

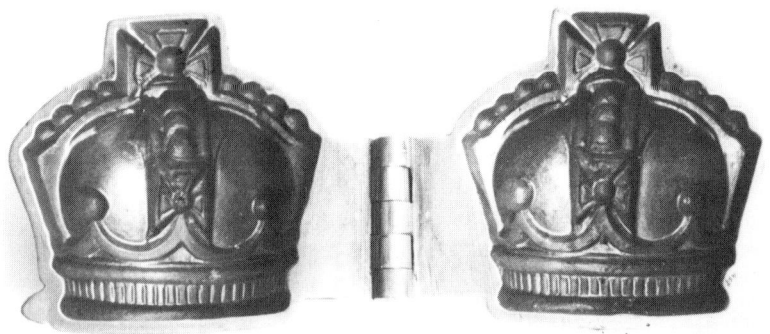

Fig. 78. Crown, 2½". Unmarked. Prime quality. $25.00 - 45.00.

Chocolate Molds

While ice cream molds are made of pewter and come in many forms and shapes, chocolate molds come in fewer subjects, but in more variety of metals. The most popular character for chocolate molds is the Easter Bunny, with Santas the next most popular. There also are Easter eggs (Figures 154 & 155), chickens (Figure 135), comic figures, animals, story-book characters, cars (Figure 152), cigars, cigarettes, etc., but these are more rare, and some, like the cigars, are less appealing or decorative.

The most common old chocolate molds are tin or tin-washed copper, but pewter and copper may also be found (Figures 98 & 103). Rare, but charming, are the primitive wooden maple sugar molds of hearts, rabbits (Figure 172), beavers, etc.

The cost of hand-processing individual ice cream shapes drove them from the market and made their pewter molds available to the collector, but chocolate figures are machine made and still very popular. A trip to the supermarket or candy store at Easter or Christmas will verify this. The tin molds are still made, but aluminum, other metals and plastic are now available. These are practical, light-weight, non-rusting, and inexpensive so the older tin and metal molds are now also in the collector's field as companies sell them and update their stock. Many molds today come from Pennsylvania, where the Hershey Chocolate Company is substituting aluminum for the old tin ones.

If you are fortunate enough to find a manufacturer or candy company which is selling out its molds, the price will be the most reasonable. Other sources are flea markets, auctions, and antique shows or dealers; not yard sales, barns, or old attics, where household antiques may sometimes be found. Prices are on the increase and will depend on many things such as condition, rarity, appeal, location, and size. A one-inch mold may be $1.00 to $2.50; a two-foot mold can run into the hundreds of dollars. A large solid chocolate rabbit sold for $250.00 at Marshall Fields at Easter. Truly a lot of chocolate!

Basically there are 3 types of chocolate molds - the two-piece held together with separate clamps, the flat one-piece or tray, and the hinged, often-banded molds latched together. The first is used for rounded solid figures; the second for solid flat pieces; and the third for hollow figures. Because the hollow figures are the sturdiest, they can be whirled or tumbled and the melted chocolate distributed by centrifugal force to make the hollow figures.

The hinged chocolate molds show signs of age or oxidation on the outside, which has been exposed to the air; while the inner area is detailed, bright and newer appearing. Since the molds were kept closed, the interior was protected.

Chocolate molds differ from ice cream molds on the outside. The pewter ice cream molds are shaped, but smooth and undetailed on the exterior; only on the interior do you see the very fine detailing (Figure 52). The metal chocolate molds are almost as detailed on the exterior as they are within.

The hinged and banded molds are heavy and often have the appearance of pewter on the outside. A little cleaning of dirt and dust often reveals the lovely soft gleam of copper showing through the plating (Figure 155). It is difficult sometimes to be sure of metal content, and errors in judgement can be made unintentionally. The buyer must make his or her own judgement of "pewter" chocolate molds.

With few exceptions ("D & Co.", Figure 54), markings on pewter ice cream molds are rather thick and raised. Markings on chocolate molds are incised like engraving on silver. Chocolate molds were and are made in many countries - Germany, England, Holland, Sweden, France, etc. as well as the United States - and there are many companies so it would be difficult to identify them. Names of companies, trade marks, model numbers, dates and countries of origin can all be found together or separately, but some molds carry no identifying marks of any kind. Markings on a mold or identification of the candy manufacturer that used it often increases the value. The illustrated molds indicate some of the markings used including Eppelsheimer & Co., (Figure 103) already familiar as an ice cream mold maker. The trade mark which appeared on many molds challenged

research, all of which proved dead ends until a mold appeared showing both the company name "Eppelsheimer" and the trade mark. The question was solved.

A trade mark resembling an open-mouthed fish is the mark of a French firm. "Trade JANION Dresden Reiche mark" is on molds marked "made in Germany." (Figures 79 & 112). T.C. Weygandt Co., New York N.Y. seems to be an importer or candy manufacturer.

The original sculptures or master molds from which molds were made might be used in different ways. A two-piece, solid chocolate mold of a rabbit riding on a chicken was found in a Chicago-area antique shop (Figure 124). The identical figure was later found in a candy store where molds from a famous Chicago candy maker were being sold out. This time the figure was used double in a hinged and clamped hollow-chocolate mold (Figure 126). Incidentally, the single figure found in the antique shop cost almost twice what the two-figured mold cost in the company sellout.

In addition, Figure 117 shows a rather wolf-nosed rabbit in a two-piece tin mold and it was also found in a modern plastic one marked "Tomric Plastics". The material may be different, but the art of the original sculptor was respected and maintained.

While rabbits are by far the most popular form of the chocolate mold, their style and subject vary greatly. Some are stylized and some are realistic, but are performing as no real-life rabbit ever did. Who ever saw a violin-playing rabbit (Figure 133), one swinging on a swing (Figure 154), one with boxing gloves ready to fight (Figure 112), or a rabbit-artist, wearing eyeglasses, with brushes and paints (Figure 127), or one whose ears are as big as his entire body? How many rabbit families have you seen out in their cars for a Sunday drive (Figure 115)? These rabbit actions and characteristics take place only in the whimsical imagination of the original artists and their sculpture. It is this subject variety which adds interest and zest to the collector's search and choice.

Fig. 79. Collection of Barbara Ray. Three-foot Santa. Supporting bands across face and mid-section have been removed. The mold is marked "Trade **Janion Reich Dresden** mark made in Germany 21335S, T.C. Weygandt New York, U.S.A.", (probably importers or candy makers). This is a rare and magnificent mold. $1,200.00 - 1,500.00

  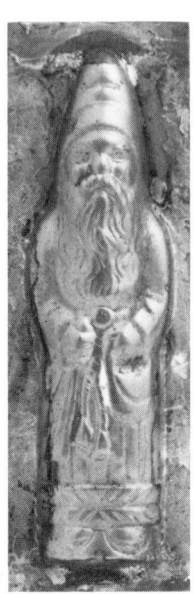

Fig. 80 - 82, left to right: Collection of Barbara Ray. Flat, one-piece Christmas Scene mold, 4½" x 8". Unmarked. $25.00 - 30.00; Flat, one-piece Santa, 4½". Unmarked. $15.00 - 20.00; Flat, one-piece, elongated Santa, 4". Unmarked. $15.00 - 20.00.

 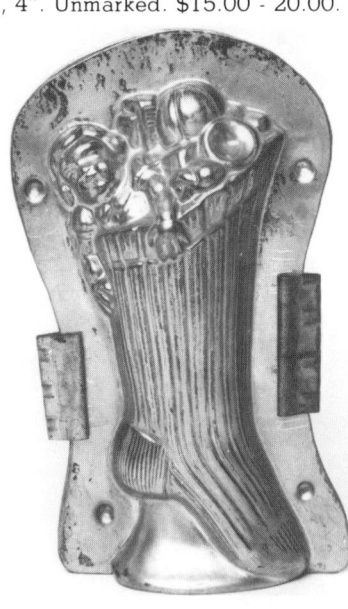

Fig. 83. Collection of Barbara Ray. Flat, one-piece mold of Santa's head. Unmarked. $15.00 - 20.00.

Fig. 84. Collection of Barbara Ray. Two-piece mold of stocking. 8". Marked "59 + 4271, Larrosh, Schw. Gmund". Rare. $95.00 - 125.00.

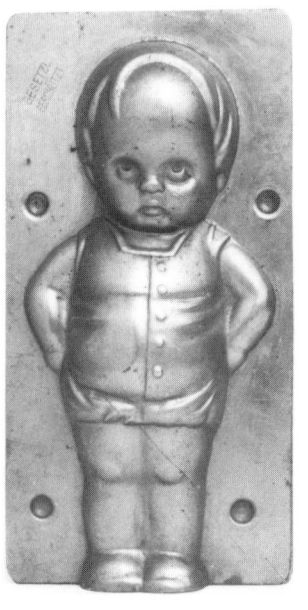

Fig. 86. Collection of Barbara Ray. Two-basket, hinged and clamped mold, 6½" x 9". Unmarked. Fine condition. $65.00 - 75.00.

Fig. 85. Two-piece, little boy mold, charmingly detailed. Marked "Gesetzl Geschutizi". Swedish. Mint condition, 5½". $35.00 - 40.00.

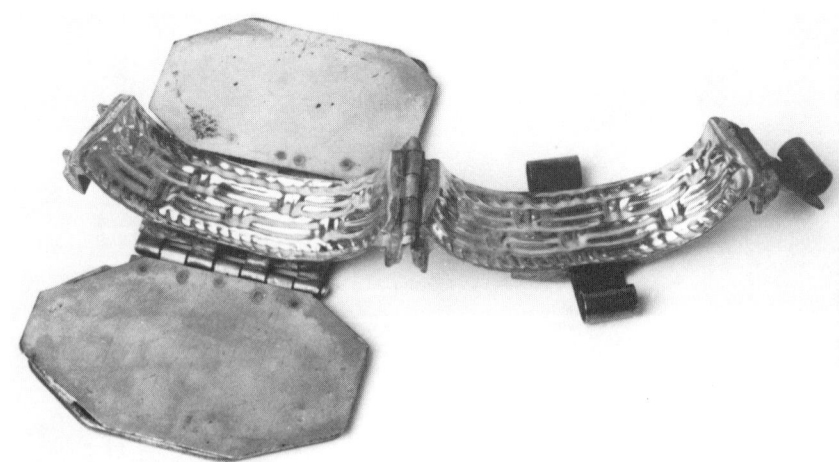

Fig. 87. Collection of Barbara Ray. Four-piece, hinged and latched basket mold. Unmarked. Condition fine. $65.00 - 75.00.

Fig. 88. Collection of Barbara Ray. Small, low basket mold, clamped. Fine condition. 1½" x 4". Unmarked. $30.00 - 35.00.

Fig. 89. Collection of Barbara Ray. Large, two-piece basket, clamped, 3" x 9". Marked "Made in U.S.A., 6068". $50.00 - 55.00.

Fig. 90. Collection of Barbara Ray. Two-piece Jack O'Lantern with heavy wire clamp. Unmarked. Excellent condition. $25.00 -35.00.

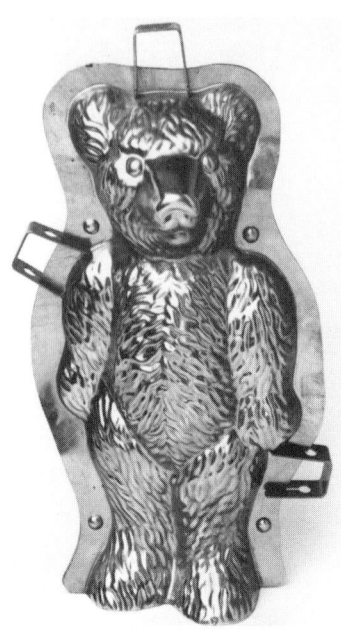

Fig. 91. Collection of Barbara Ray. Two-piece Teddy Bear with unusual clamps. Marked "2644 + 11". Rare. $125.00 - 150.00.

Fig. 92. Collection of Barbara Ray. Two piece, clamped cat. 8". Marked "8230 Made in U.S.A.". Has Eppelsheimer "top" trademark. Rare. $75.00 - 85.00.

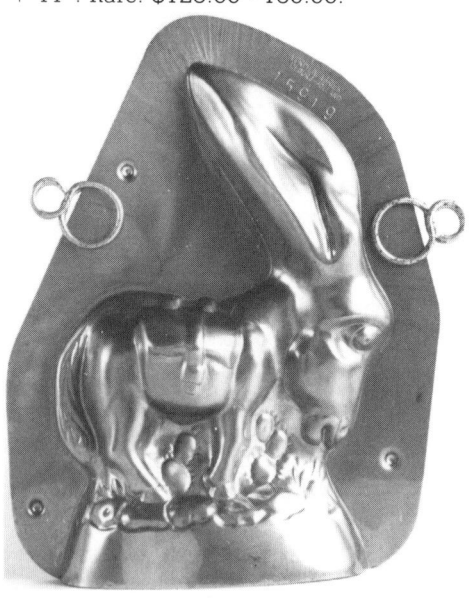

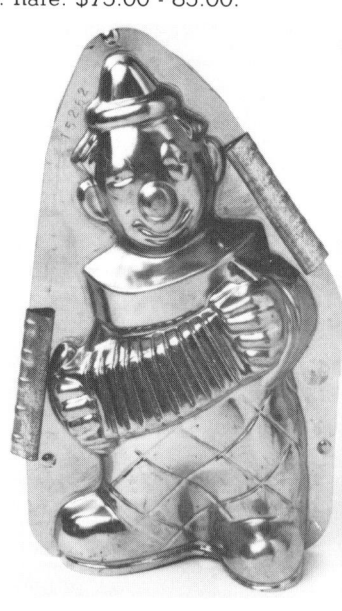

Fig. 93. Two-piece donkey with heavy wire clamps. Marked "15919, Vormenfabriek, Tilburg, Holland". 7". $25.00 - 35.00.

Fig. 94. Collection of Barbara Ray. Two-piece clown with concertina, 9". Marked "15262". $70.00 - 75.00.

Fig. 95. Collection of Barbara Ray. Two-piece, clamped mold of Snowman in top hat. 4". Rare. Fine condition. $45.00 -50.00.

Fig. 96. Half of two-piece dog head. 4". Marked "France". $10.00 - 15.00.

Fig. 97. One-piece mold of elephant, 2½" x 4". Unmarked. $10.00 - 15.00.

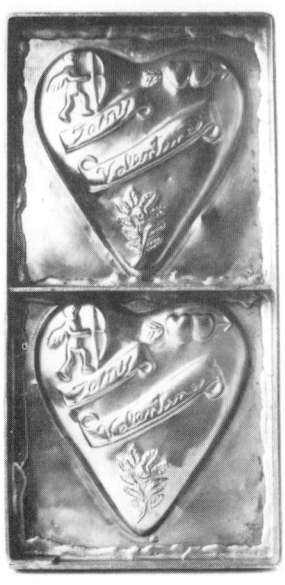

Fig. 98. One-piece copper mold of Indian, 7½". Early. From German candy factory. Unusual. Beautiful condition. $25.00 - 35.00.

Fig. 99. Collection of Barbara Ra Two-heart, two-piece mold. Heart ha cupid, flowers, and "To My Valentine Fine condition. $60.00 - 65.00.

Fig. 100. Collection of Barba Ray. Two-piece, clamped mol of heart. 9" x 9". Marked "800 Made in U.S.A." and the E pelsheimer trademark. $55.0 -65.00.

Fig. 101. One-piece mold of tin with copper bird motif. 2¼" x 4¼". $15.00 - 25.00.

Fig. 102. Collection of Barbara Ray. Three-piece, hinged and clamped turkey. Marked "Made in Germany". $40.00 - 45.00.

Fig. 103. Hinged, copper rabbit mold. Marked "Made in U.S.A., 8074" with the Eppelsheimer "top" trademark. 4". Excellent condition. Rare. $25.00 - 35.00.

Fig. 104. Two-piece mold of Easter egg with raised rabbit carrying flag. 4½". Good condition. $10.00 - 15.00.

Fig. 105. Two-piece rabbit mold with two different clamps. Unusual in smooth, undetailed form. Marked "Made in Germany". Maker's initials partly obliterated. "S ??". 5" x 5". $20.00 - 25.00.

Fig. 106. Two-piece mold of rabbit. Hinged and clamped. Marked "1749" with fish-type trademark. Smooth, undetailed. Early. Condition good. $15.00 - 25.00.

Fig. 107. Half of two-piece rabbit mold with very stylized fur details. 3½" x 4". Indentations to fit into other half of mold. Condition good. $10.00 - 20.00.

Fig. 108. Half of two-piece mold of rabbit with cane and backpack. 6". Marked "6170" and "237" with Eppelsheimer trademark. $15.00 - 25.00.

Fig. 109. Half of two-piece rabbit mold with three bumps to fit into other half. Marked "324. Made in U.S.A., 4050. Thos. Mills & Bro. Inc., Phila., Pa." with Eppelsheimer "top" trademark. $10.00 - 15.00.

Fig. 111. Two-piece mold of girl with rabbit. Clamps missing. 7". Marked "273". Smooth and undetailed. Condition fine. $45.00 - 55.00.

Fig. 110. Two-piece clamped mold of rabbit with joining indentations. Marked "6626", "1" and "13". 3¼". Condition perfect. $10.00 - 20.00.

Fig. 112. Very unusual, two-piece, clamped mold of boxing rabbit. Marked "17748 & 14, Made in Germany, 2 Trade JANION, REICH, DRESDEN". 6¼". Rare. $45.00 - 55.00.

Fig. 113. One-half of large two-piece rabbit mold. 12". $35.00 - 50.00.

Fig. 114. Large, two-piece mold of rabbit with differing clamps. 15". Unmarked except "AT" scratched in surface. Fine condition. $90.00 - 125.00.

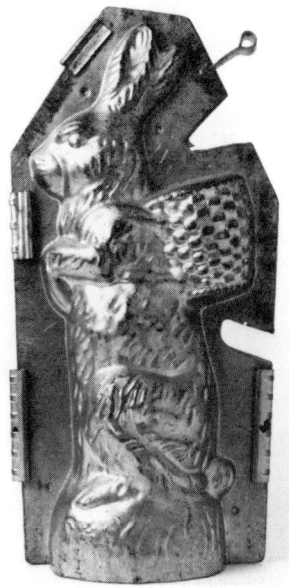

Fig. 115. Hinged and clamped two-piece mold of two cars with rabbit families. Unusual. Tin-washed copper. 4" x 8". Good condition. $45.00 - 60.00.

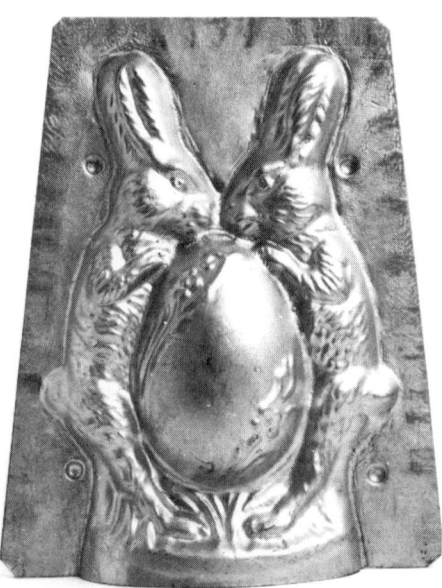

Fig. 116. Two-piece rabbit mold with indentations, but no clamps. 9". Unmarked. $45.00 - 60.00.

Fig. 117. Two-piece rabbit o[n] hind legs. 13". Unmarked. $70.00 - 75.00.

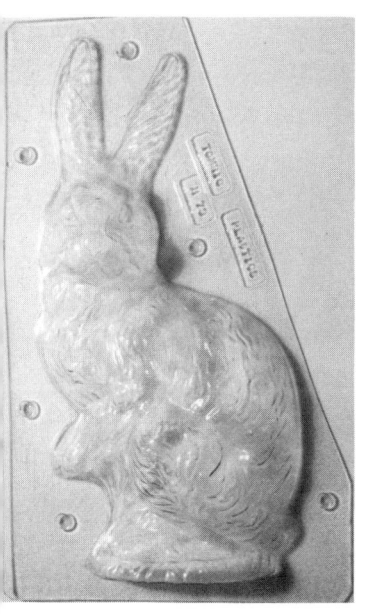

Fig. 118. Plastic mold identical to Figure 117. Front half only. Marked "Tomric Plastics 1173". $3.00 - 5.00.

Fig. 119. Two-piece clamped mold of two rabbits with basket. 7" x 7½". Marked "Made in U.S.A., 4682" with Eppelsheimer "top" trademark. $45.00 - 55.00.

Fig. 120. Half of two-piece mold of rabbit pulling cart. 4" x 8". Unmarked. Good condition. $20.00 - 25.00.

Fig. 121. Two-piece rabbit mold with clamps missing. 6" x 8½". Marked "265". $30.00 - 40.00.

Fig. 122. Two-piece rooster mold. No clamps, but indentations. Modern. Marked "312". 9". Excellent condition. $25.00 -40.00.

Fig. 123. Collection of Barbara Ray. Pair of pencils. 8½". Unmarked. $25.00 - 30.00.

Fig. 124. Two-piece, clamped mold of rabbit riding rooster. 5½" x 6". Marked "8350". Unusual. 30.00 - 40.00.

Fig. 125. Hinged and clamped, 3-piece mold of Uncle Wiggley. 4½". Bottom is broken and part missing. Unmarked. $25.00 -45.00.

Fig. 126. Hinged, clamped, and banded mold of two rabbits riding roosters. 6" x 11". Tin-washed copper. Unmarked. $35.00 - 50.00.

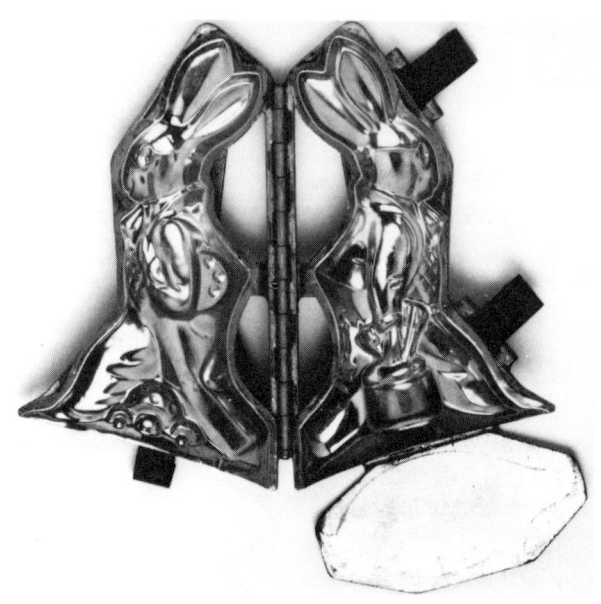

Fig. 127. Three-piece, hinged, clamped, and banded mold of bespectacled artist rabbit with paint brushes. 8". Charming and unusual. Unmarked. Fine condition. $65.00 -75.00.

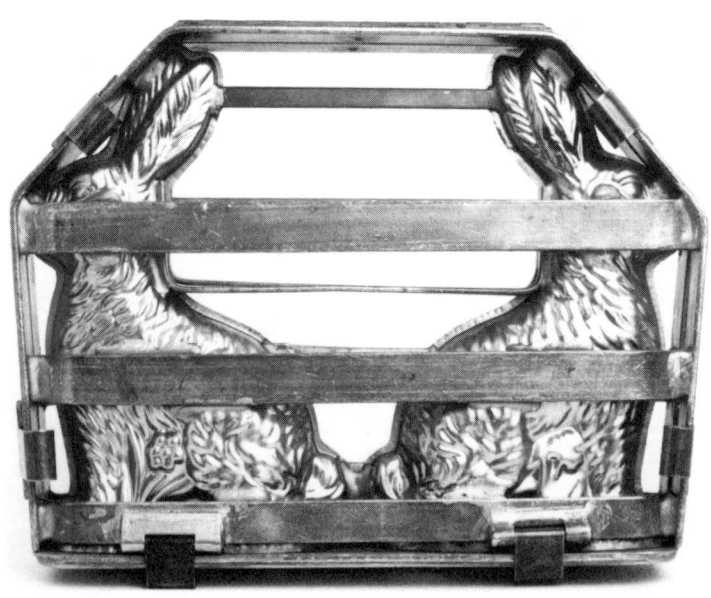

Fig. 128. Hinged, clamped, and banded mold of two rabbits. 7" x 8½". $35.00 - 50.00. Same type mold 9" x 11". $40.00 - 55.00.

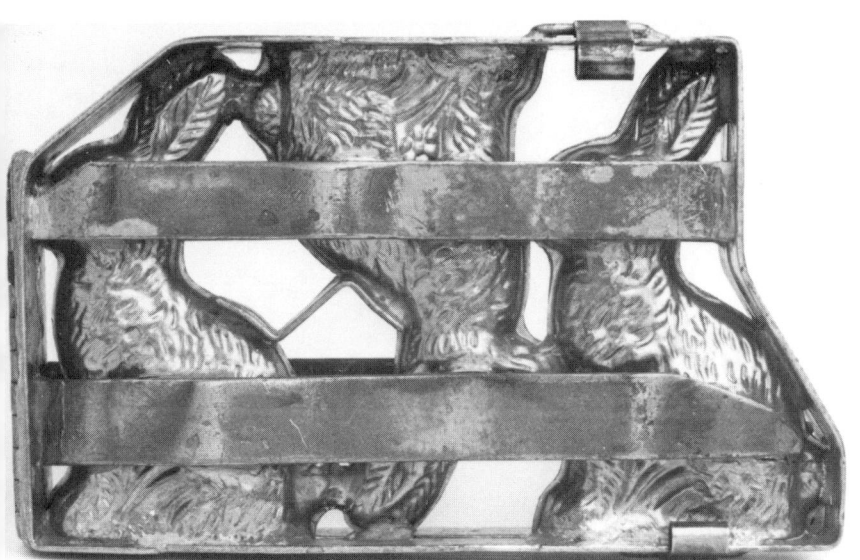

Fig. 129. Hinged, clamped, and banded two-piece mold of three rabbits. 7" x 11". One rabbit upside down to save space.) Unmarked. Unusual. Fine condition. $35.00 - 50.00.

Fig. 130. Hinged, clamped, and banded three-piece mold of three rabbits. 3½" x 7". Marked "No. 16523 and 7, D.R.G.M., T.C. Weygant Co., New York, Made in Germany". (Weygant seems to be the candy manufacturer.) One clamp broken, otherwise fine condition. Very appealing. $30.00 - 40.00.

Fig. 131. Hinged, clamped, and banded three-piece mold of running rabbit. 3" x 5". Tin-washed copper. Condition fair/good. $15.00 - 25.00.

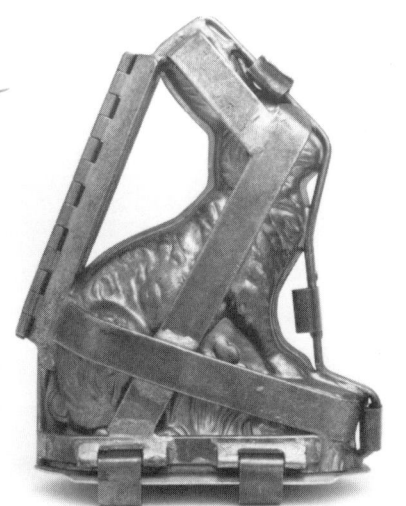

Fig. 132. Hinged, clamped, and banded three-piece mold of rabbit. 6½" x 8". Tin washed copper. Marked "437, T.C. Weygandt Co., New York, N.Y., made U.S.A.". Excellent condition. $35.00 - 45.00.

Fig. 133. Hinged, clamped and banded three-piece mold of rabbits with violins and bows. 4½" x 7". Unmarked. Condition excellent. Very charming and unusual. $45.00 - 65.00.

Fig. 134. Hinged, clamped, and banded mold of four upright rabbits. 6" x 11½". Marked "307, Germany". Either the bottom piece is missing or it is a solid chocolate mold. Early. Condition fine. $35.00 - 50.00.

Fig. 135. Hinged, banded, clamped, three-piece mold of chick. 3½" x 4". Unmarked. Early. Some rust. $10.00 - 20.00.

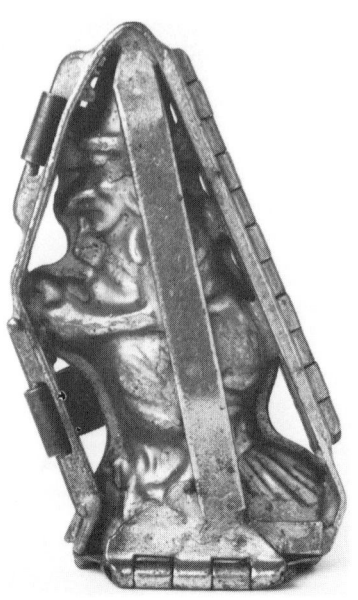

Fig. 137. Hinged and banded three-piece mold with unusual roller clamps. 6" x 9". Three charmingly dressed rabbits. Marked "Eppelsheimer & Co., N.Y., Nov. 1939, U.S. patent No. 1948 146". An exceptionally fine mold. $50.00 - 65.00.

Fig. 136. Collection of Barbara Ray. Hinged, banded, and clamped three-piece mold of witch. 6". Unmarked. Rare. $65.00 - 75.00.

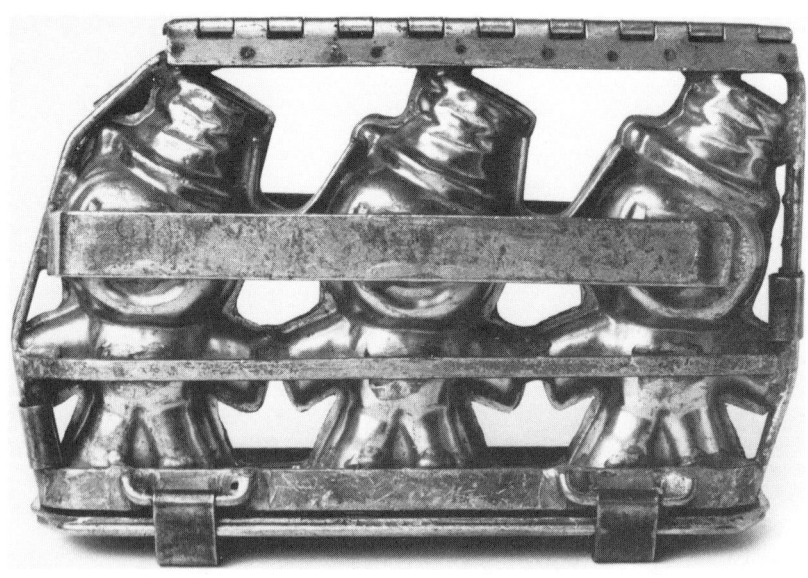

Fig. 138. Collection of Barbara Ray. Hinged, banded, and clamped three-piece mold of three scarecrows in battered top hats. 6". Unmarked. Excellent condition. Very unusual. $65.00 - 85.00.

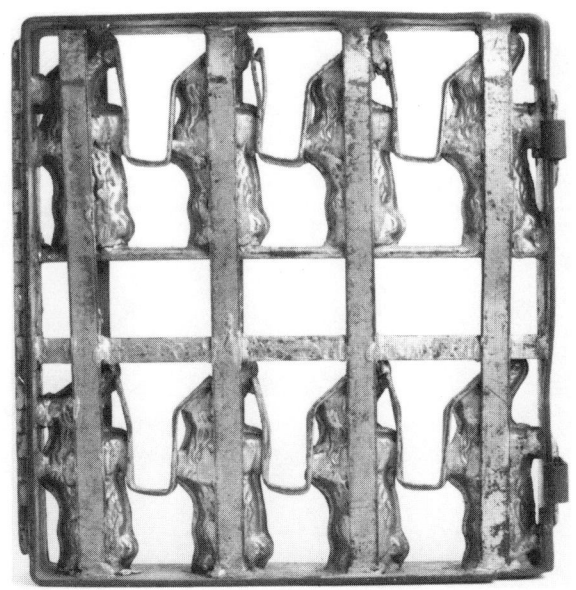

Fig. 139. Hinged, banded, and clamped two-piece, multi-figure mold of eight rabbits. Unmarked. 11" square. $35.00 - 50.00.

Fig. 140. Hinged and clamped standing rabbit with roller clamp. 4" x 9". Marked "Eppelsheimer & Co., N.Y., Dec. 1935, U.S. Pat. No. 948146". $35.00 - 50.00.

Fig. 141. Hinged, clamped, and banded two-piece mold of four rabbit houses. 2½" x 6½" x 9½". Unmarked. Very heavy construction. Probably tin-washed copper houses. Rare. $50.00 -65.00.

Fig. 142. Collection of Barbara Ray. Triple-Santa, hinged and clamped two-piece mold. 8" x 11". Unmarked. Fine condition. $65.00 - 75.00.

Fig. 143. Collection of Barbara Ray. Beautifully detailed, hinged and clamped three-piece mold of three Christmas trees. 8" x 11". Marked "Pat. Pending, trade JANION REICHE mark". Fine condition and unusual. $65.00 - 75.00.

Fig. 144. Flat lollipop mold of eight rabbits. 8" x 10". Unmarked. Rare. Fine condition. $45.00 - 55.00.

Fig. 145. Hinged and banded solid chocolate mold of six small Santas. 3" x 7½". Marked "Germany, 164". Rare. $30.00 - 45.00.

Fig. 146. Hinged, clamped, and banded two-piece mold. Four rows of four individual, candy-sized shapes - chicks, roosters, and two different rabbit poses. 6" x 8". Individual candies about 1½". A rare and charming mold in excellent condition. Unmarked. $50.00 - 75.00.

Fig. 147. Same as Figure 146, only opened to show interior detailing.

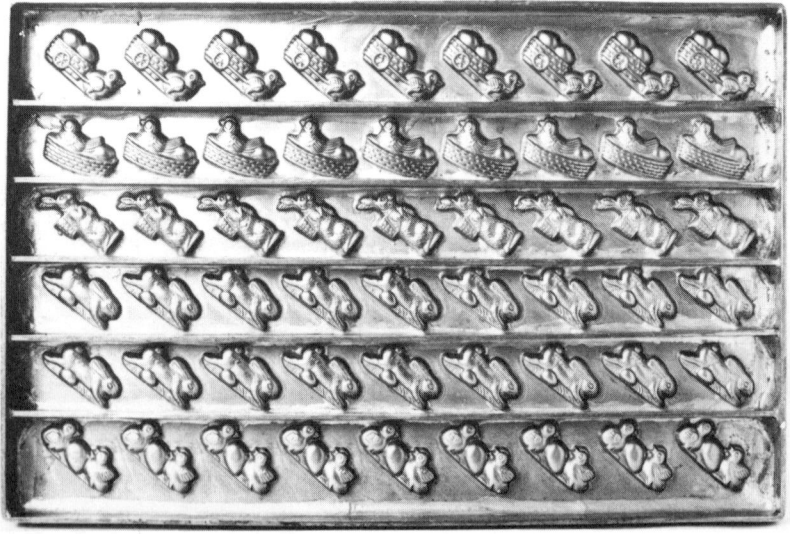

Fig. 148. Collection of Barbara Ray. Tray or plate mold. Six rows of different candies -chickens and rabbits in different poses. 11" x 17". Marked "2215.S". Excellent condition. $85.00 - 95.00.

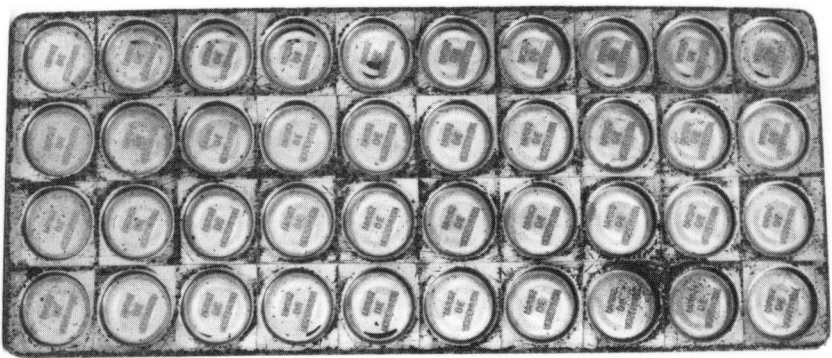

Fig. 149. Tray mold of coin-type candies which are marked "Rosemarie de Paris". 6" x 15". Marked "Eppelsheimer & Co., New York, Feb. 1944". $10.00 - 20.00.

Fig. 150. Flat mold for early Hershey bar; each section marked "Hershey". Condition only fair. Of historic interest, not much beauty. $10.00 - 20.00.

Fig. 151. Strips of molds to make individual candies from Schraft Company. 15". Good condition. $3.00 - 5.00.

Fig. 152. Flat mold of sedan, four-door car with trunk. Mint condition. 3" x 5". $5.00 - 10.00.

Fig. 153. Flat scenic mold. Landscape with rabbit pulling cart and sign, reading "5 miles to go". Mint condition. 5" x 7½". Unusual. $15.00 - 30.00.

Fig. 154. Hinged and clamped Easter egg with landscape and rabbit on each side. Pewter. 3" x 5" x 7". Charming. Fine condition. $70.00 - 85.00.

Fig. 155. Hinged, clamped, and heavily banded Easter egg with rabbit scene and scalloped edge. 5" x 6" x 9". Tin-washed copper. (Copper has worn through the plating.) Good condition. $40.00 - 50.00.

Hard Candy or Barley Sugar Molds

Of interest, but of less decorative value and appeal, are hard-candy molds. Their exteriors have not the smooth shapeliness of the pewter ice cream molds, nor the detail of tin or copper chocolate molds. They are smooth metal strips or lumps on the outside, so only by separating the pieces can you tell what form the mold is. These molds are neither hinged nor clamped as chocolate or ice cream molds are. The heavy pieces have extrusions on one side which fit into corresponding indentations on the other so that the two or three pieces (Figure 157) are held solidly together. Small strips may have two, three or four forms on the interior (Figure 158). Larger molds 6 to 8 inches high are only one or two forms used for lollipops or candy images.

Some hard-candy molds have model numbers. The larger ones may be marked "L" and "R" on the two pieces, presumably for left and right. Makers marks are not usually found.

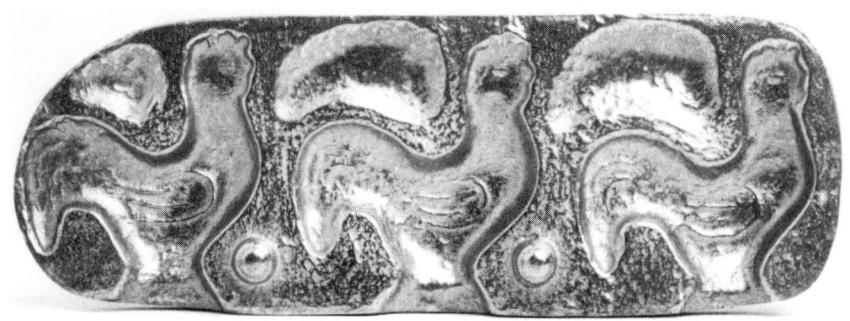

Fig. 156. Half of mold of three roosters with bumps to fit dents on other half. Excellent condition. $10.00 - 15.00.

Fig. 157. Half of fine mold of three chickens on nests. 2" x 7". Shaped indentations to fit protrusions on other half. Fine design. Fine condition. $15.00 - 20.00.

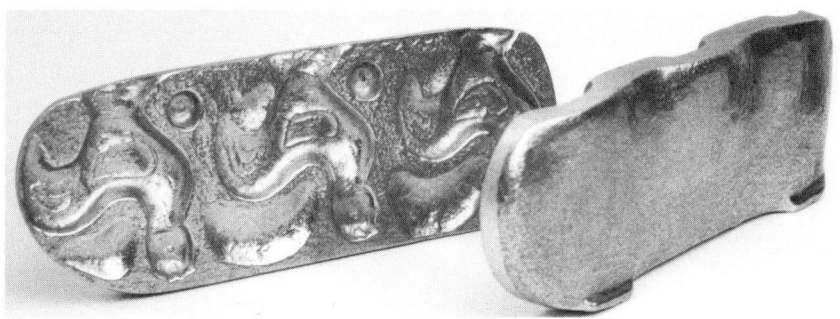

Fig. 158. Two parts of mold of three roosters, showing detailed interior and very smooth exterior. 2" x 5". Fine condition. $15.00 - 25.00.

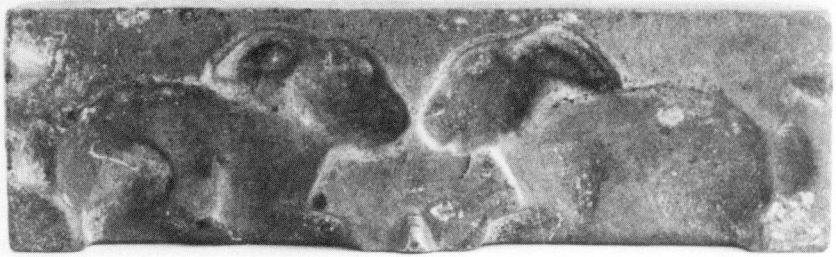

Fig. 159. Mold of two rabbits. 1" x 4". Shaped triangles fit into each other to give solidity. Rare. Fine condition. $15.00 - 25.00.

Fig. 160. Three-piece, miniature fluted basket mold. (Piece fitted into top to make hole of handle). 1¾" x 2¾". Small piece in top has one joint; other two pieces have two and three at opposite ends. Unusual. Mint condition. $20.00 - 35.00.

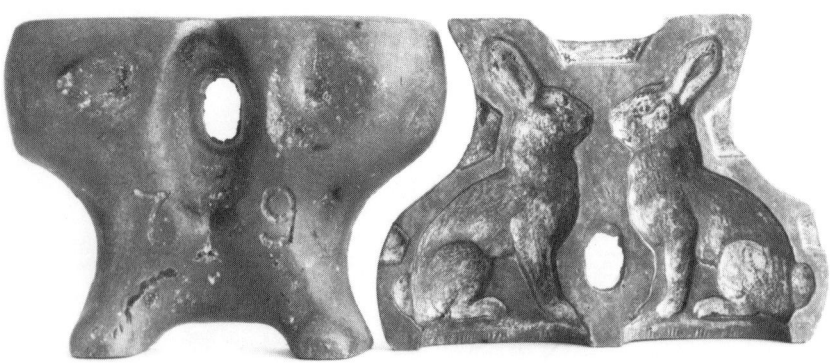

Fig. 161. Interior and exterior of two-rabbit mold. 4½" x 6". Marked "6-L" on both sides. Very heavy. Fine condition. $35.00 - 45.00.

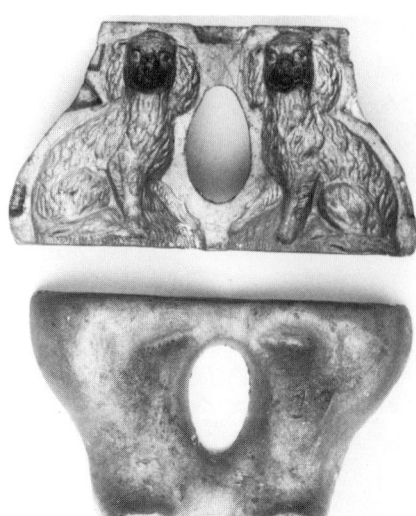

Fig. 162. Stag mold. Small piece between antlers missing. Raised "I" on each side. 3½" x 5". $35.00 - 45.00.

Fig. 163. Two-piece mold of Staffordshire dogs. 4" x 8". Marked "17" on each side. Rare. $45.00 - 60.00.

Cake Molds or Pans

Other molds for confections are cake pans. Cake batter was placed in the forms, and the cake when baked rose to fill the mold. Griswald made rabbits and lambs of heavy, black cast iron marked with the company name (Figure 164). An unmarked copy of the rabbit in base metal has also been found and a newer hammered aluminum lamb similar to the Griswald lamb. A twelve-inch, standing Santa (Figure 165) is made of cast aluminum and is sometimes mistaken as a pewter ice cream mold, for which it could probably be used. The metal is lighter weight and shinier than pewter.

The molds are two separate pieces with rings extending from the sides which are bolted together. Bolts are often lost and are missing from those illustrated. Not now collectible, (but probably explanatory of earlier cast iron molds now becoming scarce and collectible) are the modern, light-weight, aluminum cake molds now on the market priced at few dollars (Figure 169).

Fig. 164. Two-piece, cast iron cake mold of rabbit. 9" x 11". Marked "Griswald Mfg. Co., Erie, Pa". $60.00 - 95.00.

Fig. 165. Two-piece, cast-aluminum mold of Santa with his pack of toys. Marked "Hello Kiddies!!" 12". $75.00 - 85.00.

Fig. 166. Two-piece, cast-aluminum mold of lamb marked "Baker's Coconut." 8" x 12". $50.00 - 75.00.

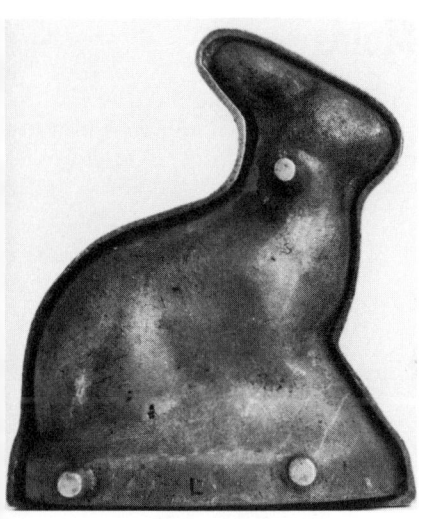

Fig. 167. Two-piece mold of rabbit. 6½" x 7". One side marked "L", the other "R". $25.00 - 35.00.

Fig. 168. Cake mold, but could be for chocolate. 6½" x 7". $10.00 - 15.00.

Fig. 169. Modern, light-weight aluminum rabbit mold complete with directions and recipes. 8" x 10". Still available. $5.00.

Unusual Molds

Probably used for making stiff gelatinous candy is the mold in Figure 170, a long geared shaft on which is imposed a brass cylinder with four indented rows of figures, two of acorns and two of strawberries. Evidently the cylinder revolved, cutting out shapes.

Fig. 170. Geared, cylindrical mold with two rows of acorns and two of strawberries on solid brass cylinder. Unusual. Meticulously made. Fine condition. $25.00 -35.00.

Fig. 171. Collection of Barbara Ray. Unusual, four-piece mold to make ice cream turkey loaf. Tin-washed copper. Good condition. $65.00 -75.00.

Fig. 172. Two-piece wooden maple-sugar rabbit mold. 1 ³⁄₄" x 2". Two pegs. Marked "Germany". $25.00 - 35.00.

Fascination Of and Uses For Collections

While searching for molds and chatting with dealers, the collector becomes increasingly aware that these collectibles have a special lure. A man in Wisconsin and a doctor in Massachusetts have shelf-lined rooms for their collections. A Massachusetts couple with over 100 ice cream molds carries a list when antiquing to avoid buying duplicates. A grandmother has increased two kitchen shelves to a whole kitchen wall full. Some antique dealers have molds squirreled away, and loathe to part with them. One dealer calls them better investments than stocks and bonds.

Some collectors use their molds as they were intended - for ice cream figures and candy, but there are also other uses. Some homemakers use the small fruits and flowers to shape butter pats and the larger ones to shape cheese hors d'oeuvres. A dealer suggested using the two parts of the heavy hard-candy molds for book ends. A rectangular ice cream mold hinged like a box with a flowered top (Figure 36) or a honor playing-card design makes an interesting pewter trinket box.

Whether for some practical use, for decoration, for investment, or just for the fun of searching and collecting, molds are interesting and popular.

Bibliography

McClinton, Katharine Morrison, "Antiques Past and Present", Part VI Pewter Chapter 23, "Ice Cream Molds".

Walcott, Duncan B., "Pewter Ice Cream Molds", *The Spinning Wheel* magazine, Sept. 1965.

Walcott, Duncan B., "Pewter Ice Cream Molds in Table or Centerpiece Size", Photos by Julius Greenfield, *The Spinning Wheel* magazine, January-February 1974.